DREAM
JOURNAL
workbook

A Beginner's Guided Dream Diary for Lucid Dreaming & Dream Interpretation

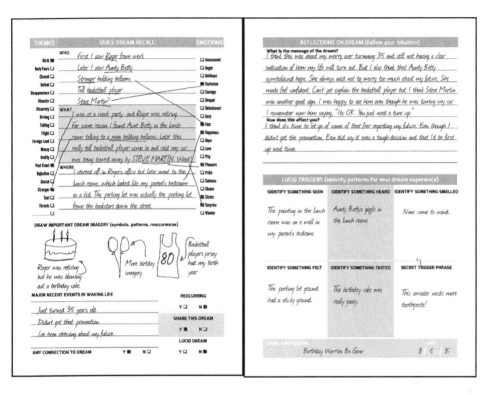

THEMES

Birth, Body Fears, Chased, Defeat, Disappearance, Disaster, Discovery, Driving, Falling, Flight, Foreign Land, Money, Nudity, Past Event, Rejection, Sexual, Stranger, Test, Threats

QUICK DREAM RECALL

WHO
First I saw Roger from work
Later I saw Aunty Betty
Stranger holding balloons
Tall basketball player
Steve Martin?

WHAT
I was at a work party and Roger was retiring.
For some reason I found Aunt Betty in the lunch room talking to a man holding balloons. Later this really tall basketball player came in and said my car was being towed away by STEVE MARTIN! What!

WHERE
I started off in Roger's office but later went to the lunch room, which looked like my parent's bedroom as a kid. The parking lot was actually the parking lot from the bookstore down the street.

EMOTIONS
Amusement, Anger, Boldness, Confusion, Courage, Despair, Detachment, Envy, Fear, Happiness, Hope, Love, Pity, Pleasure, Pride, Sadness, Shame, Stress, Surprise, Wonder

DRAW IMPORTANT DREAM IMAGERY (symbols, patterns, reoccurrences)

Roger was retiring but he was blowing out a birthday cake.

More birthday imagery

80

Basketball player's jersey had my birth year

MAJOR RECENT EVENTS IN WAKING LIFE
Just turned 35 years old.
Didn't get that promotion.
I've been stressing about my future.

ANY CONNECTION TO DREAM   Y ☒ N ☐

RECURRING   Y ☐ N ☒

SHARE THIS DREAM   Y ☒ N ☐

LUCID DREAM   Y ☐ N ☒

REFLECTIONS ON DREAM (follow your intuition)

What is the message of the dream?
I think this was about my worry over turning 35 and still not having a clear indication of how my life will turn out. But I also think that Aunty Betty symbolized hope. She always said not to worry too much about my future. She made feel confident. Can't yet explain the basketball player but I think Steve Martin was another good sign. I was happy to see him even though he was towing my car. I remember now him saying, "It's OK. You just need a tune up."

How does this affect you?
I think it's time to let go of some of that fear regarding my future. Even though I didn't get the promotion, Erin did say it was a tough decision and that I'd be first up next time.

LUCID TRIGGERS (identify patterns for next dream experience)

IDENTIFY SOMETHING SEEN
The painting in the lunch room was on a wall in my parent's bedroom.

IDENTIFY SOMETHING HEARD
Aunty Betty's giggle in the lunch room.

IDENTIFY SOMETHING SMELLED
None come to mind.

IDENTIFY SOMETHING FELT
The parking lot ground had a sticky ground.

IDENTIFY SOMETHING TASTED
The birthday cake was really gooey.

SECRET TRIGGER PHRASE
This sweater needs more toothpaste!

Birthday Worries Be Gone   8   5   15

A full description on how to use this journal can be found at the back of this book

WHO

Birth ☐
Body Fears ☐
Chased ☐
Defeat ☐
Disappearance ☐
Disaster ☐
Discovery ☐
Driving ☐
Falling ☐
Flight ☐
Foreign Land ☐
Money ☐
Nudity ☐
Past Event ☐
Rejection ☐
Sexual ☐
Stranger ☑
Test ☐
Threats ☐
☑

My Girlfriend, Devanshi and her Male friend.

WHAT

He came up and held her from behind and she let him, So I got mad and he and I got in a fist fight and he lost but devanshi was SO MAD!

WHERE

Don't Know.

Amusement ☐
Anger ☑
Boldness ☐
Confusion ☑
Courage ☐
Despair ☑
Detachment ☐
Envy ☑
Fear ☐
Happiness ☐
Hope ☑
Love ☑
Pity ☐
Pleasure ☐
Pride ☐
Sadness ☑
Shame ☐
Stress ☐
Surprise ☑
Wonder ☐

DRAW IMPORTANT DREAM IMAGERY (symbols, patterns, reoccurrences)

MAJOR RECENT EVENTS IN WAKING LIFE

Devashi Recently Left for the next 3 Months!

RECURRING

Y ☐   N ☑

SHARE THIS DREAM

Y ☐   N ☑

LUCID DREAM

Y ☐   N ☑

ANY CONNECTION TO DREAM   Y ☐   N ☑

REFLECTIONS ON DREAM (follow your intuition)

What is the message of the dream?

That devanshi will always protect everyone else except me and nothing that other guys do is ever wrong in her eyes.

How does this affect you?

It makes me mad.

LUCID TRIGGERS (identify patterns for next dream experience)

IDENTIFY SOMETHING SEEN

Devanshi
Male Friend
Blood

IDENTIFY SOMETHING HEARD

"OK Lets Go"
"He's just a friend"

IDENTIFY SOMETHING SMELLED

IDENTIFY SOMETHING FELT

Anger

IDENTIFY SOMETHING TASTED

SECRET TRIGGER PHRASE

"OK Lets Go"
"He's just a friend"

NAME YOUR DREAM

Devanshi's Male Friend

DATE

06 / 06 / 17

THEMES | QUICK DREAM RECALL | EMOTIONS

WHO My dad, My sister? Tony, Mia V., Random Indian? Jershawn, J'nique Ronan??

WHAT I taught Tony how to play music on guitar, walked to work w/ dad and sis to catch expensive ferri. Friends were taking a test and professor singled me out.

WHERE My house, Ferri Station, Classroom?

Themes:
- [ ] Birth
- [ ] Body Fears
- [ ] Chased
- [ ] Defeat
- [ ] Disappearance
- [ ] Disaster
- [ ] Discovery
- [ ] Driving
- [ ] Falling
- [ ] Flight
- [ ] Foreign Land
- [ ] Money
- [ ] Nudity
- [ ] Past Event
- [ ] Rejection
- [ ] Sexual
- [x] Stranger
- [x] Test
- [ ] Threats
- [ ] ________

Emotions:
- [ ] Amusement
- [ ] Anger
- [ ] Boldness
- [x] Confusion
- [x] Courage
- [ ] Despair
- [ ] Detachment
- [ ] Envy
- [ ] Fear
- [ ] Happiness
- [ ] Hope
- [ ] Love
- [ ] Pity
- [ ] Pleasure
- [ ] Pride
- [ ] Sadness
- [ ] Shame
- [ ] Stress
- [ ] Surprise
- [ ] Wonder

DRAW IMPORTANT DREAM IMAGERY (symbols, patterns, reoccurrences)

MAJOR RECENT EVENTS IN WAKING LIFE

I haven't attended college yet but ALL my friends are almost finished.

ANY CONNECTION TO DREAM Y [x] N [ ]

RECURRING Y [ ] N [x]

SHARE THIS DREAM Y [ ] N [x]

LUCID DREAM Y [ ] N [x]

What is the message of the dream?

I need to start College because I'm so behind. (I had to go to work but I wanted to stay in the class but I couldn't)

How does this affect you?

It makes me feel useless and it makes me despair. I feel stupid.

IDENTIFY SOMETHING SEEN

Ferri, tickets, movie, guitar teacher, desks,

IDENTIFY SOMETHING HEARD

Harry Potter theme song.
will you help me at work?
I'll be $20 -dad.
for a ticket but you'll save $50.

IDENTIFY SOMETHING SMELLED

IDENTIFY SOMETHING FELT

Confusion.

IDENTIFY SOMETHING TASTED

SECRET TRIGGER PHRASE

NAME YOUR DREAM

Ferri School

DATE

06 06 17

WHO

THEMES		EMOTIONS
Birth ❑		❑ Amusement
Body Fears ❑		❑ Anger
Chased ❑		❑ Boldness
Defeat ❑		❑ Confusion
Disappearance ❑		❑ Courage
Disaster ❑		❑ Despair
Discovery ❑	WHAT	❑ Detachment
Driving ❑		❑ Envy
Falling ❑		❑ Fear
Flight ❑		❑ Happiness
Foreign Land ❑		❑ Hope
Money ❑		❑ Love
Nudity ❑		❑ Pity
Past Event ❑	WHERE	❑ Pleasure
Rejection ❑		❑ Pride
Sexual ❑		❑ Sadness
Stranger ❑		❑ Shame
Test ❑		❑ Stress
Threats ❑		❑ Surprise
_____ ❑		❑ Wonder

DRAW IMPORTANT DREAM IMAGERY (symbols, patterns, reoccurrences)

MAJOR RECENT EVENTS IN WAKING LIFE

RECURRING

Y ❑　　　N ❑

SHARE THIS DREAM

Y ❑　　　N ❑

LUCID DREAM

ANY CONNECTION TO DREAM　　Y ❑　　N ❑　　　Y ❑　　　N ❑

REFLECTIONS ON DREAM (follow your intuition)

What is the message of the dream?

_____

_____

_____

_____

_____

_____

How does this affect you?

_____

_____

_____

_____

_____

LUCID TRIGGERS (identify patterns for next dream experience)

IDENTIFY SOMETHING SEEN	IDENTIFY SOMETHING HEARD	IDENTIFY SOMETHING SMELLED
IDENTIFY SOMETHING FELT	IDENTIFY SOMETHING TASTED	SECRET TRIGGER PHRASE

NAME YOUR DREAM

DATE / /

WHO

Birth ❏	———————————————	❏ Amusement
Body Fears ❏		❏ Anger
Chased ❏		❏ Boldness
Defeat ❏		❏ Confusion
Disappearance ❏		❏ Courage
Disaster ❏		❏ Despair
Discovery ❏	WHAT	❏ Detachment
Driving ❏		❏ Envy
Falling ❏		❏ Fear
Flight ❏		❏ Happiness
Foreign Land ❏		❏ Hope
Money ❏		❏ Love
Nudity ❏		❏ Pity
Past Event ❏	WHERE	❏ Pleasure
Rejection ❏		❏ Pride
Sexual ❏		❏ Sadness
Stranger ❏		❏ Shame
Test ❏		❏ Stress
Threats ❏		❏ Surprise
_____ ❏		❏ Wonder

DRAW IMPORTANT DREAM IMAGERY (symbols, patterns, reoccurrences)

MAJOR RECENT EVENTS IN WAKING LIFE

RECURRING

Y ❏   N ❏

SHARE THIS DREAM

Y ❏   N ❏

LUCID DREAM

ANY CONNECTION TO DREAM   Y ❏   N ❏   Y ❏   N ❏

What is the message of the dream?

_____

_____

_____

_____

_____

_____

How does this affect you?

_____

_____

_____

_____

_____

LUCID TRIGGERS (identify patterns for next dream experience)

IDENTIFY SOMETHING SEEN	IDENTIFY SOMETHING HEARD	IDENTIFY SOMETHING SMELLED
IDENTIFY SOMETHING FELT	IDENTIFY SOMETHING TASTED	SECRET TRIGGER PHRASE

NAME YOUR DREAM

DATE
/   /

WHO

Birth ❑ _____ ❑ Amusement

Body Fears ❑ _____ ❑ Anger

Chased ❑ _____ ❑ Boldness

Defeat ❑ _____ ❑ Confusion

Disappearance ❑ _____ ❑ Courage

Disaster ❑ _____ ❑ Despair

Discovery ❑ WHAT ❑ Detachment

Driving ❑ _____ ❑ Envy

Falling ❑ _____ ❑ Fear

Flight ❑ _____ ❑ Happiness

Foreign Land ❑ _____ ❑ Hope

Money ❑ _____ ❑ Love

Nudity ❑ _____ ❑ Pity

Past Event ❑ WHERE ❑ Pleasure

Rejection ❑ _____ ❑ Pride

Sexual ❑ _____ ❑ Sadness

Stranger ❑ _____ ❑ Shame

Test ❑ _____ ❑ Stress

Threats ❑ _____ ❑ Surprise

_____ ❑ ❑ Wonder

DRAW IMPORTANT DREAM IMAGERY (symbols, patterns, reoccurrences)

MAJOR RECENT EVENTS IN WAKING LIFE

RECURRING

Y ❑   N ❑

_____

_____   **SHARE THIS DREAM**

_____   Y ❑   N ❑

_____

LUCID DREAM

_____

ANY CONNECTION TO DREAM   Y ❑   N ❑   Y ❑   N ❑

REFLECTIONS ON DREAM (follow your intuition)

What is the message of the dream?

_____

_____

_____

_____

_____

_____

How does this affect you?

_____

_____

_____

_____

LUCID TRIGGERS (identify patterns for next dream experience)

IDENTIFY SOMETHING SEEN	IDENTIFY SOMETHING HEARD	IDENTIFY SOMETHING SMELLED
IDENTIFY SOMETHING FELT	IDENTIFY SOMETHING TASTED	SECRET TRIGGER PHRASE

NAME YOUR DREAM

DATE
/ /

WHO

Birth ❑	_____	❑ Amusement
Body Fears ❑		❑ Anger
Chased ❑		❑ Boldness
Defeat ❑		❑ Confusion
Disappearance ❑		❑ Courage
Disaster ❑		❑ Despair
Discovery ❑	WHAT	❑ Detachment
Driving ❑		❑ Envy
Falling ❑		❑ Fear
Flight ❑		❑ Happiness
Foreign Land ❑		❑ Hope
Money ❑		❑ Love
Nudity ❑		❑ Pity
Past Event ❑	WHERE	❑ Pleasure
Rejection ❑		❑ Pride
Sexual ❑		❑ Sadness
Stranger ❑		❑ Shame
Test ❑		❑ Stress
Threats ❑		❑ Surprise
_____ ❑		❑ Wonder

DRAW IMPORTANT DREAM IMAGERY (symbols, patterns, reoccurrences)

MAJOR RECENT EVENTS IN WAKING LIFE

RECURRING

Y ❑   N ❑

SHARE THIS DREAM

Y ❑   N ❑

LUCID DREAM

ANY CONNECTION TO DREAM   Y ❑   N ❑   Y ❑   N ❑

REFLECTIONS ON DREAM (follow your intuition)

What is the message of the dream?

_____

_____

_____

_____

_____

_____

_____

How does this affect you?

_____

_____

_____

_____

LUCID TRIGGERS (identify patterns for next dream experience)

IDENTIFY SOMETHING SEEN	IDENTIFY SOMETHING HEARD	IDENTIFY SOMETHING SMELLED
IDENTIFY SOMETHING FELT	IDENTIFY SOMETHING TASTED	SECRET TRIGGER PHRASE

NAME YOUR DREAM

DATE

/ /

WHO

THEMES		EMOTIONS
Birth ❑		❑ Amusement
Body Fears ❑		❑ Anger
Chased ❑		❑ Boldness
Defeat ❑		❑ Confusion
Disappearance ❑		❑ Courage
Disaster ❑		❑ Despair
Discovery ❑	**WHAT**	❑ Detachment
Driving ❑		❑ Envy
Falling ❑		❑ Fear
Flight ❑		❑ Happiness
Foreign Land ❑		❑ Hope
Money ❑		❑ Love
Nudity ❑		❑ Pity
Past Event ❑	**WHERE**	❑ Pleasure
Rejection ❑		❑ Pride
Sexual ❑		❑ Sadness
Stranger ❑		❑ Shame
Test ❑		❑ Stress
Threats ❑		❑ Surprise
_____ ❑		❑ Wonder

DRAW IMPORTANT DREAM IMAGERY (symbols, patterns, reoccurrences)

MAJOR RECENT EVENTS IN WAKING LIFE

RECURRING

Y ❑   N ❑

SHARE THIS DREAM

Y ❑   N ❑

LUCID DREAM

ANY CONNECTION TO DREAM   Y ❑   N ❑   Y ❑   N ❑

REFLECTIONS ON DREAM (follow your intuition)

What is the message of the dream?

_____
_____
_____
_____
_____
_____
_____

How does this affect you?

_____
_____
_____
_____

LUCID TRIGGERS (identify patterns for next dream experience)

IDENTIFY SOMETHING SEEN   **IDENTIFY SOMETHING HEARD**   **IDENTIFY SOMETHING SMELLED**

IDENTIFY SOMETHING FELT   **IDENTIFY SOMETHING TASTED**   **SECRET TRIGGER PHRASE**

NAME YOUR DREAM   **DATE**
/   /

WHO

Theme	Emotion
Birth ☐	☐ Amusement
Body Fears ☐	☐ Anger
Chased ☐	☐ Boldness
Defeat ☐	☐ Confusion
Disappearance ☐	☐ Courage
Disaster ☐	☐ Despair
Discovery ☐	☐ Detachment
Driving ☐	☐ Envy
Falling ☐	☐ Fear
Flight ☐	☐ Happiness
Foreign Land ☐	☐ Hope
Money ☐	☐ Love
Nudity ☐	☐ Pity
Past Event ☐	☐ Pleasure
Rejection ☐	☐ Pride
Sexual ☐	☐ Sadness
Stranger ☐	☐ Shame
Test ☐	☐ Stress
Threats ☐	☐ Surprise
_____ ☐	☐ Wonder

WHAT

WHERE

DRAW IMPORTANT DREAM IMAGERY (symbols, patterns, reoccurrences)

MAJOR RECENT EVENTS IN WAKING LIFE

RECURRING

Y ☐   N ☐

SHARE THIS DREAM

Y ☐   N ☐

LUCID DREAM

ANY CONNECTION TO DREAM   Y ☐   N ☐   Y ☐   N ☐

What is the message of the dream?

_____

_____

_____

_____

_____

How does this affect you?

_____

_____

_____

_____

LUCID TRIGGERS (identify patterns for next dream experience)

IDENTIFY SOMETHING SEEN	IDENTIFY SOMETHING HEARD	IDENTIFY SOMETHING SMELLED
IDENTIFY SOMETHING FELT	IDENTIFY SOMETHING TASTED	SECRET TRIGGER PHRASE

NAME YOUR DREAM

DATE

/ /

WHO

Birth ❑	❑ Amusement
Body Fears ❑	❑ Anger
Chased ❑	❑ Boldness
Defeat ❑	❑ Confusion
Disappearance ❑	❑ Courage
Disaster ❑	❑ Despair
Discovery ❑	❑ Detachment
Driving ❑	❑ Envy
Falling ❑	❑ Fear
Flight ❑	❑ Happiness
Foreign Land ❑	❑ Hope
Money ❑	❑ Love
Nudity ❑	❑ Pity
Past Event ❑	❑ Pleasure
Rejection ❑	❑ Pride
Sexual ❑	❑ Sadness
Stranger ❑	❑ Shame
Test ❑	❑ Stress
Threats ❑	❑ Surprise
_____ ❑	❑ Wonder

WHAT

WHERE

DRAW IMPORTANT DREAM IMAGERY (symbols, patterns, reoccurrences)

MAJOR RECENT EVENTS IN WAKING LIFE

RECURRING

Y ❑   N ❑

SHARE THIS DREAM

Y ❑   N ❑

LUCID DREAM

ANY CONNECTION TO DREAM   Y ❑   N ❑   Y ❑   N ❑

REFLECTIONS ON DREAM (follow your intuition)

What is the message of the dream?

_____

_____

_____

_____

_____

_____

How does this affect you?

_____

_____

_____

_____

LUCID TRIGGERS (identify patterns for next dream experience)

IDENTIFY SOMETHING SEEN   **IDENTIFY SOMETHING HEARD**   **IDENTIFY SOMETHING SMELLED**

IDENTIFY SOMETHING FELT   **IDENTIFY SOMETHING TASTED**   **SECRET TRIGGER PHRASE**

NAME YOUR DREAM   **DATE**

/   /

WHO
_____

Birth ❏
Body Fears ❏
Chased ❏
Defeat ❏
Disappearance ❏
Disaster ❏
Discovery ❏   WHAT
Driving ❏
Falling ❏
Flight ❏
Foreign Land ❏
Money ❏
Nudity ❏
Past Event ❏   WHERE
Rejection ❏
Sexual ❏
Stranger ❏
Test ❏
Threats ❏
_____ ❏

❏ Amusement
❏ Anger
❏ Boldness
❏ Confusion
❏ Courage
❏ Despair
❏ Detachment
❏ Envy
❏ Fear
❏ Happiness
❏ Hope
❏ Love
❏ Pity
❏ Pleasure
❏ Pride
❏ Sadness
❏ Shame
❏ Stress
❏ Surprise
❏ Wonder

DRAW IMPORTANT DREAM IMAGERY (symbols, patterns, reoccurrences)

MAJOR RECENT EVENTS IN WAKING LIFE

RECURRING

Y ❏   N ❏

SHARE THIS DREAM

Y ❏   N ❏

LUCID DREAM

ANY CONNECTION TO DREAM   Y ❏   N ❏   Y ❏   N ❏

What is the message of the dream?

_____

_____

_____

_____

_____

_____

How does this affect you?

_____

_____

_____

_____

LUCID TRIGGERS (identify patterns for next dream experience)

IDENTIFY SOMETHING SEEN	IDENTIFY SOMETHING HEARD	IDENTIFY SOMETHING SMELLED
IDENTIFY SOMETHING FELT	IDENTIFY SOMETHING TASTED	SECRET TRIGGER PHRASE

NAME YOUR DREAM

DATE

/ /

WHO

Birth ❏		❏ Amusement
Body Fears ❏		❏ Anger
Chased ❏		❏ Boldness
Defeat ❏		❏ Confusion
Disappearance ❏		❏ Courage
Disaster ❏		❏ Despair
Discovery ❏	WHAT	❏ Detachment
Driving ❏		❏ Envy
Falling ❏		❏ Fear
Flight ❏		❏ Happiness
Foreign Land ❏		❏ Hope
Money ❏		❏ Love
Nudity ❏		❏ Pity
Past Event ❏	WHERE	❏ Pleasure
Rejection ❏		❏ Pride
Sexual ❏		❏ Sadness
Stranger ❏		❏ Shame
Test ❏		❏ Stress
Threats ❏		❏ Surprise
_____ ❏		❏ Wonder

DRAW IMPORTANT DREAM IMAGERY (symbols, patterns, reoccurrences)

MAJOR RECENT EVENTS IN WAKING LIFE

RECURRING

Y ❏   N ❏

SHARE THIS DREAM

Y ❏   N ❏

LUCID DREAM

ANY CONNECTION TO DREAM   Y ❏   N ❏   Y ❏   N ❏

REFLECTIONS ON DREAM (follow your intuition)

What is the message of the dream?

_____

_____

_____

_____

_____

_____

How does this affect you?

_____

_____

_____

_____

LUCID TRIGGERS (identify patterns for next dream experience)

IDENTIFY SOMETHING SEEN	IDENTIFY SOMETHING HEARD	IDENTIFY SOMETHING SMELLED
IDENTIFY SOMETHING FELT	IDENTIFY SOMETHING TASTED	SECRET TRIGGER PHRASE

NAME YOUR DREAM

DATE / /

WHO

Birth ❑		❑ Amusement
Body Fears ❑		❑ Anger
Chased ❑		❑ Boldness
Defeat ❑		❑ Confusion
Disappearance ❑		❑ Courage
Disaster ❑		❑ Despair
Discovery ❑	WHAT	❑ Detachment
Driving ❑		❑ Envy
Falling ❑		❑ Fear
Flight ❑		❑ Happiness
Foreign Land ❑		❑ Hope
Money ❑		❑ Love
Nudity ❑		❑ Pity
Past Event ❑	WHERE	❑ Pleasure
Rejection ❑		❑ Pride
Sexual ❑		❑ Sadness
Stranger ❑		❑ Shame
Test ❑		❑ Stress
Threats ❑		❑ Surprise
_____ ❑		❑ Wonder

DRAW IMPORTANT DREAM IMAGERY (symbols, patterns, reoccurrences)

MAJOR RECENT EVENTS IN WAKING LIFE

RECURRING

Y ❑   N ❑

SHARE THIS DREAM

Y ❑   N ❑

LUCID DREAM

ANY CONNECTION TO DREAM   Y ❑   N ❑   Y ❑   N ❑

What is the message of the dream?

_____

_____

_____

_____

_____

_____

How does this affect you?

_____

_____

_____

_____

_____

LUCID TRIGGERS (identify patterns for next dream experience)

IDENTIFY SOMETHING SEEN	IDENTIFY SOMETHING HEARD	IDENTIFY SOMETHING SMELLED
IDENTIFY SOMETHING FELT	IDENTIFY SOMETHING TASTED	SECRET TRIGGER PHRASE

NAME YOUR DREAM   DATE

/   /

WHO

Birth ❑	_____	❑ Amusement
Body Fears ❑	_____	❑ Anger
Chased ❑	_____	❑ Boldness
Defeat ❑	_____	❑ Confusion
Disappearance ❑	_____	❑ Courage
Disaster ❑		❑ Despair
Discovery ❑	WHAT	❑ Detachment
Driving ❑	_____	❑ Envy
Falling ❑	_____	❑ Fear
Flight ❑	_____	❑ Happiness
Foreign Land ❑	_____	❑ Hope
Money ❑	_____	❑ Love
Nudity ❑	_____	❑ Pity
Past Event ❑	WHERE	❑ Pleasure
Rejection ❑	_____	❑ Pride
Sexual ❑	_____	❑ Sadness
Stranger ❑	_____	❑ Shame
Test ❑	_____	❑ Stress
Threats ❑	_____	❑ Surprise
_____ ❑		❑ Wonder

DRAW IMPORTANT DREAM IMAGERY (symbols, patterns, reoccurrences)

MAJOR RECENT EVENTS IN WAKING LIFE

RECURRING

Y ❑   N ❑

SHARE THIS DREAM

Y ❑   N ❑

LUCID DREAM

ANY CONNECTION TO DREAM   Y ❑   N ❑   Y ❑   N ❑

What is the message of the dream?

_____

_____

_____

_____

_____

_____

How does this affect you?

_____

_____

_____

_____

LUCID TRIGGERS (identify patterns for next dream experience)

IDENTIFY SOMETHING SEEN	IDENTIFY SOMETHING HEARD	IDENTIFY SOMETHING SMELLED
IDENTIFY SOMETHING FELT	IDENTIFY SOMETHING TASTED	SECRET TRIGGER PHRASE

NAME YOUR DREAM

DATE

/   /

WHO

Birth ❑	_____	❑ Amusement
Body Fears ❑		❑ Anger
Chased ❑		❑ Boldness
Defeat ❑		❑ Confusion
Disappearance ❑		❑ Courage
Disaster ❑		❑ Despair
Discovery ❑	WHAT	❑ Detachment
Driving ❑		❑ Envy
Falling ❑		❑ Fear
Flight ❑		❑ Happiness
Foreign Land ❑		❑ Hope
Money ❑		❑ Love
Nudity ❑		❑ Pity
Past Event ❑	WHERE	❑ Pleasure
Rejection ❑		❑ Pride
Sexual ❑		❑ Sadness
Stranger ❑		❑ Shame
Test ❑		❑ Stress
Threats ❑		❑ Surprise
_____ ❑		❑ Wonder

DRAW IMPORTANT DREAM IMAGERY (symbols, patterns, reoccurrences)

MAJOR RECENT EVENTS IN WAKING LIFE

_____

_____

_____

_____

_____

RECURRING

Y ❑   N ❑

SHARE THIS DREAM

Y ❑   N ❑

LUCID DREAM

Y ❑   N ❑

ANY CONNECTION TO DREAM   Y ❑   N ❑

REFLECTIONS ON DREAM (follow your intuition)

What is the message of the dream?

_____

_____

_____

_____

_____

How does this affect you?

_____

_____

_____

_____

LUCID TRIGGERS (identify patterns for next dream experience)

IDENTIFY SOMETHING SEEN	IDENTIFY SOMETHING HEARD	IDENTIFY SOMETHING SMELLED
IDENTIFY SOMETHING FELT	IDENTIFY SOMETHING TASTED	SECRET TRIGGER PHRASE

NAME YOUR DREAM

DATE

/   /

WHO

Birth ❑		❑ Amusement
Body Fears ❑		❑ Anger
Chased ❑		❑ Boldness
Defeat ❑		❑ Confusion
Disappearance ❑		❑ Courage
Disaster ❑		❑ Despair
Discovery ❑	WHAT	❑ Detachment
Driving ❑		❑ Envy
Falling ❑		❑ Fear
Flight ❑		❑ Happiness
Foreign Land ❑		❑ Hope
Money ❑		❑ Love
Nudity ❑		❑ Pity
Past Event ❑	WHERE	❑ Pleasure
Rejection ❑		❑ Pride
Sexual ❑		❑ Sadness
Stranger ❑		❑ Shame
Test ❑		❑ Stress
Threats ❑		❑ Surprise
_____ ❑		❑ Wonder

DRAW IMPORTANT DREAM IMAGERY (symbols, patterns, reoccurrences)

MAJOR RECENT EVENTS IN WAKING LIFE

RECURRING

Y ❑   N ❑

SHARE THIS DREAM

Y ❑   N ❑

LUCID DREAM

ANY CONNECTION TO DREAM   Y ❑   N ❑   Y ❑   N ❑

REFLECTIONS ON DREAM (follow your intuition)

What is the message of the dream?

How does this affect you?

LUCID TRIGGERS (identify patterns for next dream experience)

IDENTIFY SOMETHING SEEN

IDENTIFY SOMETHING HEARD

IDENTIFY SOMETHING SMELLED

IDENTIFY SOMETHING FELT

IDENTIFY SOMETHING TASTED

SECRET TRIGGER PHRASE

NAME YOUR DREAM

DATE

/ /

WHO

Birth ❑	
Body Fears ❑	
Chased ❑	
Defeat ❑	
Disappearance ❑	
Disaster ❑	
Discovery ❑	WHAT
Driving ❑	
Falling ❑	
Flight ❑	
Foreign Land ❑	
Money ❑	
Nudity ❑	
Past Event ❑	WHERE
Rejection ❑	
Sexual ❑	
Stranger ❑	
Test ❑	
Threats ❑	
_____ ❑	

❑ Amusement
❑ Anger
❑ Boldness
❑ Confusion
❑ Courage
❑ Despair
❑ Detachment
❑ Envy
❑ Fear
❑ Happiness
❑ Hope
❑ Love
❑ Pity
❑ Pleasure
❑ Pride
❑ Sadness
❑ Shame
❑ Stress
❑ Surprise
❑ Wonder

DRAW IMPORTANT DREAM IMAGERY (symbols, patterns, reoccurrences)

MAJOR RECENT EVENTS IN WAKING LIFE

RECURRING

Y ❑   N ❑

SHARE THIS DREAM

Y ❑   N ❑

LUCID DREAM

ANY CONNECTION TO DREAM   Y ❑   N ❑   Y ❑   N ❑

What is the message of the dream?

_____

_____

_____

_____

_____

_____

How does this affect you?

_____

_____

_____

_____

LUCID TRIGGERS (identify patterns for next dream experience)

IDENTIFY SOMETHING SEEN	IDENTIFY SOMETHING HEARD	IDENTIFY SOMETHING SMELLED

IDENTIFY SOMETHING FELT	IDENTIFY SOMETHING TASTED	SECRET TRIGGER PHRASE

NAME YOUR DREAM

DATE
/ /

WHO

Birth ❏		❏ Amusement
Body Fears ❏		❏ Anger
Chased ❏		❏ Boldness
Defeat ❏		❏ Confusion
Disappearance ❏		❏ Courage
Disaster ❏		❏ Despair
Discovery ❏	WHAT	❏ Detachment
Driving ❏		❏ Envy
Falling ❏		❏ Fear
Flight ❏		❏ Happiness
Foreign Land ❏		❏ Hope
Money ❏		❏ Love
Nudity ❏		❏ Pity
Past Event ❏	WHERE	❏ Pleasure
Rejection ❏		❏ Pride
Sexual ❏		❏ Sadness
Stranger ❏		❏ Shame
Test ❏		❏ Stress
Threats ❏		❏ Surprise
_____ ❏		❏ Wonder

DRAW IMPORTANT DREAM IMAGERY (symbols, patterns, reoccurrences)

MAJOR RECENT EVENTS IN WAKING LIFE

RECURRING

Y ❏   N ❏

SHARE THIS DREAM

Y ❏   N ❏

LUCID DREAM

ANY CONNECTION TO DREAM   Y ❏   N ❏   Y ❏   N ❏

REFLECTIONS ON DREAM (follow your intuition)

What is the message of the dream?

_____

_____

_____

_____

_____

How does this affect you?

_____

_____

_____

_____

LUCID TRIGGERS (identify patterns for next dream experience)

IDENTIFY SOMETHING SEEN   **IDENTIFY SOMETHING HEARD**   **IDENTIFY SOMETHING SMELLED**

IDENTIFY SOMETHING FELT   **IDENTIFY SOMETHING TASTED**   **SECRET TRIGGER PHRASE**

NAME YOUR DREAM   **DATE**

/ /

WHO

Birth ❑	❑ Amusement
Body Fears ❑	❑ Anger
Chased ❑	❑ Boldness
Defeat ❑	❑ Confusion
Disappearance ❑	❑ Courage
Disaster ❑	❑ Despair
Discovery ❑	❑ Detachment
Driving ❑	❑ Envy
Falling ❑	❑ Fear
Flight ❑	❑ Happiness
Foreign Land ❑	❑ Hope
Money ❑	❑ Love
Nudity ❑	❑ Pity
Past Event ❑	❑ Pleasure
Rejection ❑	❑ Pride
Sexual ❑	❑ Sadness
Stranger ❑	❑ Shame
Test ❑	❑ Stress
Threats ❑	❑ Surprise
_____ ❑	❑ Wonder

WHAT

WHERE

DRAW IMPORTANT DREAM IMAGERY (symbols, patterns, reoccurrences)

MAJOR RECENT EVENTS IN WAKING LIFE

RECURRING

Y ❑   N ❑

SHARE THIS DREAM

Y ❑   N ❑

LUCID DREAM

ANY CONNECTION TO DREAM   Y ❑   N ❑   Y ❑   N ❑

What is the message of the dream?

_____
_____
_____
_____
_____
_____

How does this affect you?

_____
_____
_____
_____

LUCID TRIGGERS (identify patterns for next dream experience)

IDENTIFY SOMETHING SEEN   **IDENTIFY SOMETHING HEARD**   **IDENTIFY SOMETHING SMELLED**

IDENTIFY SOMETHING FELT   **IDENTIFY SOMETHING TASTED**   **SECRET TRIGGER PHRASE**

NAME YOUR DREAM   **DATE**

/   /

WHO

THEMES		EMOTIONS
Birth ❑		❑ Amusement
Body Fears ❑		❑ Anger
Chased ❑		❑ Boldness
Defeat ❑		❑ Confusion
Disappearance ❑		❑ Courage
Disaster ❑		❑ Despair
Discovery ❑	**WHAT**	❑ Detachment
Driving ❑		❑ Envy
Falling ❑		❑ Fear
Flight ❑		❑ Happiness
Foreign Land ❑		❑ Hope
Money ❑		❑ Love
Nudity ❑		❑ Pity
Past Event ❑	**WHERE**	❑ Pleasure
Rejection ❑		❑ Pride
Sexual ❑		❑ Sadness
Stranger ❑		❑ Shame
Test ❑		❑ Stress
Threats ❑		❑ Surprise
_____ ❑		❑ Wonder

DRAW IMPORTANT DREAM IMAGERY (symbols, patterns, reoccurrences)

MAJOR RECENT EVENTS IN WAKING LIFE

RECURRING

Y ❑   N ❑

SHARE THIS DREAM

Y ❑   N ❑

LUCID DREAM

ANY CONNECTION TO DREAM   Y ❑   N ❑   Y ❑   N ❑

REFLECTIONS ON DREAM (follow your intuition)

What is the message of the dream?

_____

_____

_____

_____

_____

How does this affect you?

_____

_____

_____

_____

LUCID TRIGGERS (identify patterns for next dream experience)

IDENTIFY SOMETHING SEEN	IDENTIFY SOMETHING HEARD	IDENTIFY SOMETHING SMELLED
IDENTIFY SOMETHING FELT	IDENTIFY SOMETHING TASTED	SECRET TRIGGER PHRASE

NAME YOUR DREAM   DATE

/   /

WHO

Birth ❑	❑ Amusement
Body Fears ❑	❑ Anger
Chased ❑	❑ Boldness
Defeat ❑	❑ Confusion
Disappearance ❑	❑ Courage
Disaster ❑	❑ Despair
Discovery ❑	❑ Detachment
Driving ❑	❑ Envy
Falling ❑	❑ Fear
Flight ❑	❑ Happiness
Foreign Land ❑	❑ Hope
Money ❑	❑ Love
Nudity ❑	❑ Pity
Past Event ❑	❑ Pleasure
Rejection ❑	❑ Pride
Sexual ❑	❑ Sadness
Stranger ❑	❑ Shame
Test ❑	❑ Stress
Threats ❑	❑ Surprise
_____ ❑	❑ Wonder

WHAT

WHERE

DRAW IMPORTANT DREAM IMAGERY (symbols, patterns, reoccurrences)

MAJOR RECENT EVENTS IN WAKING LIFE

RECURRING

Y ❑   N ❑

SHARE THIS DREAM

Y ❑   N ❑

LUCID DREAM

ANY CONNECTION TO DREAM   Y ❑   N ❑   Y ❑   N ❑

REFLECTIONS ON DREAM (follow your intuition)

What is the message of the dream?

How does this affect you?

LUCID TRIGGERS (identify patterns for next dream experience)

IDENTIFY SOMETHING SEEN   **IDENTIFY SOMETHING HEARD**   **IDENTIFY SOMETHING SMELLED**

IDENTIFY SOMETHING FELT   **IDENTIFY SOMETHING TASTED**   **SECRET TRIGGER PHRASE**

NAME YOUR DREAM   DATE

/ /

WHO

Birth ❑		❑ Amusement
Body Fears ❑		❑ Anger
Chased ❑		❑ Boldness
Defeat ❑		❑ Confusion
Disappearance ❑		❑ Courage
Disaster ❑		❑ Despair
Discovery ❑	WHAT	❑ Detachment
Driving ❑		❑ Envy
Falling ❑		❑ Fear
Flight ❑		❑ Happiness
Foreign Land ❑		❑ Hope
Money ❑		❑ Love
Nudity ❑		❑ Pity
Past Event ❑	WHERE	❑ Pleasure
Rejection ❑		❑ Pride
Sexual ❑		❑ Sadness
Stranger ❑		❑ Shame
Test ❑		❑ Stress
Threats ❑		❑ Surprise
_____ ❑		❑ Wonder

DRAW IMPORTANT DREAM IMAGERY (symbols, patterns, reoccurrences)

MAJOR RECENT EVENTS IN WAKING LIFE

RECURRING

Y ❑   N ❑

SHARE THIS DREAM

Y ❑   N ❑

LUCID DREAM

ANY CONNECTION TO DREAM   Y ❑   N ❑   Y ❑   N ❑

What is the message of the dream?

_____

_____

_____

_____

_____

How does this affect you?

_____

_____

_____

_____

LUCID TRIGGERS (identify patterns for next dream experience)

IDENTIFY SOMETHING SEEN	IDENTIFY SOMETHING HEARD	IDENTIFY SOMETHING SMELLED

IDENTIFY SOMETHING FELT	IDENTIFY SOMETHING TASTED	SECRET TRIGGER PHRASE

NAME YOUR DREAM

DATE

/ /

WHO

Theme		Emotion
Birth ❑		❑ Amusement
Body Fears ❑		❑ Anger
Chased ❑		❑ Boldness
Defeat ❑		❑ Confusion
Disappearance ❑		❑ Courage
Disaster ❑		❑ Despair
Discovery ❑	WHAT	❑ Detachment
Driving ❑		❑ Envy
Falling ❑		❑ Fear
Flight ❑		❑ Happiness
Foreign Land ❑		❑ Hope
Money ❑		❑ Love
Nudity ❑		❑ Pity
Past Event ❑	WHERE	❑ Pleasure
Rejection ❑		❑ Pride
Sexual ❑		❑ Sadness
Stranger ❑		❑ Shame
Test ❑		❑ Stress
Threats ❑		❑ Surprise
_____ ❑		❑ Wonder

DRAW IMPORTANT DREAM IMAGERY (symbols, patterns, reoccurrences)

MAJOR RECENT EVENTS IN WAKING LIFE

RECURRING

Y ❑   N ❑

SHARE THIS DREAM

Y ❑   N ❑

LUCID DREAM

ANY CONNECTION TO DREAM   Y ❑   N ❑   Y ❑   N ❑

REFLECTIONS ON DREAM (follow your intuition)

What is the message of the dream?

_____

_____

_____

_____

_____

_____

How does this affect you?

_____

_____

_____

_____

LUCID TRIGGERS (identify patterns for next dream experience)

IDENTIFY SOMETHING SEEN **IDENTIFY SOMETHING HEARD** **IDENTIFY SOMETHING SMELLED**

IDENTIFY SOMETHING FELT **IDENTIFY SOMETHING TASTED** **SECRET TRIGGER PHRASE**

NAME YOUR DREAM **DATE**

/ /

WHO

Birth ❏

Body Fears ❏

Chased ❏

Defeat ❏

Disappearance ❏

Disaster ❏

Discovery ❏   WHAT

Driving ❏

Falling ❏

Flight ❏

Foreign Land ❏

Money ❏

Nudity ❏

Past Event ❏   WHERE

Rejection ❏

Sexual ❏

Stranger ❏

Test ❏

Threats ❏

_____ ❏

❏ Amusement

❏ Anger

❏ Boldness

❏ Confusion

❏ Courage

❏ Despair

❏ Detachment

❏ Envy

❏ Fear

❏ Happiness

❏ Hope

❏ Love

❏ Pity

❏ Pleasure

❏ Pride

❏ Sadness

❏ Shame

❏ Stress

❏ Surprise

❏ Wonder

DRAW IMPORTANT DREAM IMAGERY (symbols, patterns, reoccurrences)

MAJOR RECENT EVENTS IN WAKING LIFE

RECURRING

Y ❏   N ❏

SHARE THIS DREAM

Y ❏   N ❏

LUCID DREAM

ANY CONNECTION TO DREAM   Y ❏   N ❏   Y ❏   N ❏

What is the message of the dream?

_____

_____

_____

_____

_____

_____

How does this affect you?

_____

_____

_____

_____

LUCID TRIGGERS (identify patterns for next dream experience)

IDENTIFY SOMETHING SEEN	IDENTIFY SOMETHING HEARD	IDENTIFY SOMETHING SMELLED

IDENTIFY SOMETHING FELT	IDENTIFY SOMETHING TASTED	SECRET TRIGGER PHRASE

NAME YOUR DREAM

DATE

/ /

WHO

Birth ☐		☐ Amusement
Body Fears ☐		☐ Anger
Chased ☐		☐ Boldness
Defeat ☐		☐ Confusion
Disappearance ☐		☐ Courage
Disaster ☐		☐ Despair
Discovery ☐	**WHAT**	☐ Detachment
Driving ☐		☐ Envy
Falling ☐		☐ Fear
Flight ☐		☐ Happiness
Foreign Land ☐		☐ Hope
Money ☐		☐ Love
Nudity ☐		☐ Pity
Past Event ☐	**WHERE**	☐ Pleasure
Rejection ☐		☐ Pride
Sexual ☐		☐ Sadness
Stranger ☐		☐ Shame
Test ☐		☐ Stress
Threats ☐		☐ Surprise
_____ ☐		☐ Wonder

DRAW IMPORTANT DREAM IMAGERY (symbols, patterns, reoccurrences)

MAJOR RECENT EVENTS IN WAKING LIFE

RECURRING

Y ☐   N ☐

SHARE THIS DREAM

Y ☐   N ☐

LUCID DREAM

ANY CONNECTION TO DREAM   Y ☐   N ☐   Y ☐   N ☐

REFLECTIONS ON DREAM (follow your intuition)

What is the message of the dream?

_____

_____

_____

_____

_____

_____

How does this affect you?

_____

_____

_____

_____

LUCID TRIGGERS (identify patterns for next dream experience)

IDENTIFY SOMETHING SEEN   **IDENTIFY SOMETHING HEARD**   **IDENTIFY SOMETHING SMELLED**

IDENTIFY SOMETHING FELT   **IDENTIFY SOMETHING TASTED**   **SECRET TRIGGER PHRASE**

NAME YOUR DREAM   **DATE**

/   /

WHO

Theme		Emotion
Birth ❑		❑ Amusement
Body Fears ❑		❑ Anger
Chased ❑		❑ Boldness
Defeat ❑		❑ Confusion
Disappearance ❑		❑ Courage
Disaster ❑		❑ Despair
Discovery ❑	WHAT	❑ Detachment
Driving ❑		❑ Envy
Falling ❑		❑ Fear
Flight ❑		❑ Happiness
Foreign Land ❑		❑ Hope
Money ❑		❑ Love
Nudity ❑		❑ Pity
Past Event ❑	WHERE	❑ Pleasure
Rejection ❑		❑ Pride
Sexual ❑		❑ Sadness
Stranger ❑		❑ Shame
Test ❑		❑ Stress
Threats ❑		❑ Surprise
_____ ❑		❑ Wonder

DRAW IMPORTANT DREAM IMAGERY (symbols, patterns, reoccurrences)

MAJOR RECENT EVENTS IN WAKING LIFE

RECURRING

Y ❑   N ❑

SHARE THIS DREAM

Y ❑   N ❑

LUCID DREAM

ANY CONNECTION TO DREAM   Y ❑   N ❑   Y ❑   N ❑

REFLECTIONS ON DREAM (follow your intuition)

What is the message of the dream?

_____

_____

_____

_____

_____

_____

How does this affect you?

_____

_____

_____

_____

LUCID TRIGGERS (identify patterns for next dream experience)

IDENTIFY SOMETHING SEEN

IDENTIFY SOMETHING HEARD

IDENTIFY SOMETHING SMELLED

IDENTIFY SOMETHING FELT

IDENTIFY SOMETHING TASTED

SECRET TRIGGER PHRASE

NAME YOUR DREAM

DATE

/   /

WHO

THEMES		EMOTIONS
Birth ❏		❏ Amusement
Body Fears ❏		❏ Anger
Chased ❏		❏ Boldness
Defeat ❏		❏ Confusion
Disappearance ❏		❏ Courage
Disaster ❏		❏ Despair
Discovery ❏	WHAT	❏ Detachment
Driving ❏		❏ Envy
Falling ❏		❏ Fear
Flight ❏		❏ Happiness
Foreign Land ❏		❏ Hope
Money ❏		❏ Love
Nudity ❏		❏ Pity
Past Event ❏	WHERE	❏ Pleasure
Rejection ❏		❏ Pride
Sexual ❏		❏ Sadness
Stranger ❏		❏ Shame
Test ❏		❏ Stress
Threats ❏		❏ Surprise
_____ ❏		❏ Wonder

DRAW IMPORTANT DREAM IMAGERY (symbols, patterns, reoccurrences)

MAJOR RECENT EVENTS IN WAKING LIFE

RECURRING

Y ❏   N ❏

SHARE THIS DREAM

Y ❏   N ❏

LUCID DREAM

ANY CONNECTION TO DREAM   Y ❏   N ❏   Y ❏   N ❏

What is the message of the dream?

_____

_____

_____

_____

_____

How does this affect you?

_____

_____

_____

_____

_____

LUCID TRIGGERS (identify patterns for next dream experience)

IDENTIFY SOMETHING SEEN	IDENTIFY SOMETHING HEARD	IDENTIFY SOMETHING SMELLED
IDENTIFY SOMETHING FELT	IDENTIFY SOMETHING TASTED	SECRET TRIGGER PHRASE

NAME YOUR DREAM

DATE

/ /

WHO

THEMES		EMOTIONS
Birth ❑		❑ Amusement
Body Fears ❑		❑ Anger
Chased ❑		❑ Boldness
Defeat ❑		❑ Confusion
Disappearance ❑		❑ Courage
Disaster ❑		❑ Despair
Discovery ❑	**WHAT**	❑ Detachment
Driving ❑		❑ Envy
Falling ❑		❑ Fear
Flight ❑		❑ Happiness
Foreign Land ❑		❑ Hope
Money ❑		❑ Love
Nudity ❑		❑ Pity
Past Event ❑	**WHERE**	❑ Pleasure
Rejection ❑		❑ Pride
Sexual ❑		❑ Sadness
Stranger ❑		❑ Shame
Test ❑		❑ Stress
Threats ❑		❑ Surprise
_____ ❑		❑ Wonder

DRAW IMPORTANT DREAM IMAGERY (symbols, patterns, reoccurrences)

MAJOR RECENT EVENTS IN WAKING LIFE

RECURRING

Y ❑   N ❑

SHARE THIS DREAM

Y ❑   N ❑

LUCID DREAM

ANY CONNECTION TO DREAM   Y ❑   N ❑   Y ❑   N ❑

REFLECTIONS ON DREAM (follow your intuition)

What is the message of the dream?

_____

_____

_____

_____

_____

_____

How does this affect you?

_____

_____

_____

_____

LUCID TRIGGERS (identify patterns for next dream experience)

IDENTIFY SOMETHING SEEN	IDENTIFY SOMETHING HEARD	IDENTIFY SOMETHING SMELLED
IDENTIFY SOMETHING FELT	IDENTIFY SOMETHING TASTED	SECRET TRIGGER PHRASE

NAME YOUR DREAM

DATE

/   /

WHO

Birth ☐		☐ Amusement
Body Fears ☐		☐ Anger
Chased ☐		☐ Boldness
Defeat ☐		☐ Confusion
Disappearance ☐		☐ Courage
Disaster ☐		☐ Despair
Discovery ☐	**WHAT**	☐ Detachment
Driving ☐		☐ Envy
Falling ☐		☐ Fear
Flight ☐		☐ Happiness
Foreign Land ☐		☐ Hope
Money ☐		☐ Love
Nudity ☐		☐ Pity
Past Event ☐	**WHERE**	☐ Pleasure
Rejection ☐		☐ Pride
Sexual ☐		☐ Sadness
Stranger ☐		☐ Shame
Test ☐		☐ Stress
Threats ☐		☐ Surprise
_____ ☐		☐ Wonder

DRAW IMPORTANT DREAM IMAGERY (symbols, patterns, reoccurrences)

MAJOR RECENT EVENTS IN WAKING LIFE

RECURRING

Y ☐   N ☐

SHARE THIS DREAM

Y ☐   N ☐

LUCID DREAM

ANY CONNECTION TO DREAM   Y ☐   N ☐   Y ☐   N ☐

REFLECTIONS ON DREAM (follow your intuition)

What is the message of the dream?

_____

_____

_____

_____

_____

_____

How does this affect you?

_____

_____

_____

_____

_____

LUCID TRIGGERS (identify patterns for next dream experience)

IDENTIFY SOMETHING SEEN	IDENTIFY SOMETHING HEARD	IDENTIFY SOMETHING SMELLED
IDENTIFY SOMETHING FELT	**IDENTIFY SOMETHING TASTED**	**SECRET TRIGGER PHRASE**

NAME YOUR DREAM

DATE

/ /

WHO

Birth ❏

Body Fears ❏

Chased ❏

Defeat ❏

Disappearance ❏

Disaster ❏

Discovery ❏   **WHAT**

Driving ❏

Falling ❏

Flight ❏

Foreign Land ❏

Money ❏

Nudity ❏

Past Event ❏   **WHERE**

Rejection ❏

Sexual ❏

Stranger ❏

Test ❏

Threats ❏

_____ ❏

❏ Amusement

❏ Anger

❏ Boldness

❏ Confusion

❏ Courage

❏ Despair

❏ Detachment

❏ Envy

❏ Fear

❏ Happiness

❏ Hope

❏ Love

❏ Pity

❏ Pleasure

❏ Pride

❏ Sadness

❏ Shame

❏ Stress

❏ Surprise

❏ Wonder

DRAW IMPORTANT DREAM IMAGERY (symbols, patterns, reoccurrences)

MAJOR RECENT EVENTS IN WAKING LIFE

RECURRING

Y ❏   N ❏

SHARE THIS DREAM

Y ❏   N ❏

LUCID DREAM

ANY CONNECTION TO DREAM   Y ❏   N ❏   Y ❏   N ❏

What is the message of the dream?

_____
_____
_____
_____
_____
_____

How does this affect you?

_____
_____
_____
_____

LUCID TRIGGERS (identify patterns for next dream experience)

IDENTIFY SOMETHING SEEN	IDENTIFY SOMETHING HEARD	IDENTIFY SOMETHING SMELLED
IDENTIFY SOMETHING FELT	IDENTIFY SOMETHING TASTED	SECRET TRIGGER PHRASE

NAME YOUR DREAM

DATE

/   /

WHO

Themes		Emotions
Birth ❑		❑ Amusement
Body Fears ❑		❑ Anger
Chased ❑		❑ Boldness
Defeat ❑		❑ Confusion
Disappearance ❑		❑ Courage
Disaster ❑		❑ Despair
Discovery ❑	**WHAT**	❑ Detachment
Driving ❑		❑ Envy
Falling ❑		❑ Fear
Flight ❑		❑ Happiness
Foreign Land ❑		❑ Hope
Money ❑		❑ Love
Nudity ❑		❑ Pity
Past Event ❑	**WHERE**	❑ Pleasure
Rejection ❑		❑ Pride
Sexual ❑		❑ Sadness
Stranger ❑		❑ Shame
Test ❑		❑ Stress
Threats ❑		❑ Surprise
_____ ❑		❑ Wonder

DRAW IMPORTANT DREAM IMAGERY (symbols, patterns, reoccurrences)

MAJOR RECENT EVENTS IN WAKING LIFE

RECURRING

Y ❑ 　 N ❑

SHARE THIS DREAM

Y ❑ 　 N ❑

LUCID DREAM

ANY CONNECTION TO DREAM 　 Y ❑ 　 N ❑ 　 Y ❑ 　 N ❑

REFLECTIONS ON DREAM (follow your intuition)

What is the message of the dream?

_____

_____

_____

_____

_____

How does this affect you?

_____

_____

_____

_____

LUCID TRIGGERS (identify patterns for next dream experience)

IDENTIFY SOMETHING SEEN	IDENTIFY SOMETHING HEARD	IDENTIFY SOMETHING SMELLED
IDENTIFY SOMETHING FELT	IDENTIFY SOMETHING TASTED	SECRET TRIGGER PHRASE

NAME YOUR DREAM

DATE

/ /

WHO

Birth ❑

Body Fears ❑

Chased ❑

Defeat ❑

Disappearance ❑

Disaster ❑

Discovery ❑   WHAT

Driving ❑

Falling ❑

Flight ❑

Foreign Land ❑

Money ❑

Nudity ❑

Past Event ❑   WHERE

Rejection ❑

Sexual ❑

Stranger ❑

Test ❑

Threats ❑

_____ ❑

❑ Amusement

❑ Anger

❑ Boldness

❑ Confusion

❑ Courage

❑ Despair

❑ Detachment

❑ Envy

❑ Fear

❑ Happiness

❑ Hope

❑ Love

❑ Pity

❑ Pleasure

❑ Pride

❑ Sadness

❑ Shame

❑ Stress

❑ Surprise

❑ Wonder

DRAW IMPORTANT DREAM IMAGERY (symbols, patterns, reoccurrences)

MAJOR RECENT EVENTS IN WAKING LIFE   **RECURRING**

Y ❑   N ❑

SHARE THIS DREAM

Y ❑   N ❑

LUCID DREAM

ANY CONNECTION TO DREAM   Y ❑   N ❑   Y ❑   N ❑

What is the message of the dream?

_____

_____

_____

_____

_____

_____

How does this affect you?

_____

_____

_____

_____

_____

LUCID TRIGGERS (identify patterns for next dream experience)

IDENTIFY SOMETHING SEEN	IDENTIFY SOMETHING HEARD	IDENTIFY SOMETHING SMELLED
IDENTIFY SOMETHING FELT	IDENTIFY SOMETHING TASTED	SECRET TRIGGER PHRASE

NAME YOUR DREAM   **DATE**

/   /

WHO

THEMES		EMOTIONS
Birth ❑		❑ Amusement
Body Fears ❑		❑ Anger
Chased ❑		❑ Boldness
Defeat ❑		❑ Confusion
Disappearance ❑		❑ Courage
Disaster ❑		❑ Despair
Discovery ❑	**WHAT**	❑ Detachment
Driving ❑		❑ Envy
Falling ❑		❑ Fear
Flight ❑		❑ Happiness
Foreign Land ❑		❑ Hope
Money ❑		❑ Love
Nudity ❑		❑ Pity
Past Event ❑	**WHERE**	❑ Pleasure
Rejection ❑		❑ Pride
Sexual ❑		❑ Sadness
Stranger ❑		❑ Shame
Test ❑		❑ Stress
Threats ❑		❑ Surprise
_____ ❑		❑ Wonder

DRAW IMPORTANT DREAM IMAGERY (symbols, patterns, reoccurrences)

MAJOR RECENT EVENTS IN WAKING LIFE

RECURRING

Y ❑   N ❑

SHARE THIS DREAM

Y ❑   N ❑

LUCID DREAM

ANY CONNECTION TO DREAM   Y ❑   N ❑   Y ❑   N ❑

REFLECTIONS ON DREAM (follow your intuition)

What is the message of the dream?

_____

_____

_____

_____

_____

_____

How does this affect you?

_____

_____

_____

_____

LUCID TRIGGERS (identify patterns for next dream experience)

IDENTIFY SOMETHING SEEN	IDENTIFY SOMETHING HEARD	IDENTIFY SOMETHING SMELLED
IDENTIFY SOMETHING FELT	IDENTIFY SOMETHING TASTED	SECRET TRIGGER PHRASE

NAME YOUR DREAM

DATE

/   /

WHO

Themes		Emotions
Birth ❑		❑ Amusement
Body Fears ❑		❑ Anger
Chased ❑		❑ Boldness
Defeat ❑		❑ Confusion
Disappearance ❑		❑ Courage
Disaster ❑		❑ Despair
Discovery ❑	WHAT	❑ Detachment
Driving ❑		❑ Envy
Falling ❑		❑ Fear
Flight ❑		❑ Happiness
Foreign Land ❑		❑ Hope
Money ❑		❑ Love
Nudity ❑		❑ Pity
Past Event ❑	WHERE	❑ Pleasure
Rejection ❑		❑ Pride
Sexual ❑		❑ Sadness
Stranger ❑		❑ Shame
Test ❑		❑ Stress
Threats ❑		❑ Surprise
_____ ❑		❑ Wonder

DRAW IMPORTANT DREAM IMAGERY (symbols, patterns, reoccurrences)

MAJOR RECENT EVENTS IN WAKING LIFE

RECURRING

Y ❑   N ❑

SHARE THIS DREAM

Y ❑   N ❑

LUCID DREAM

ANY CONNECTION TO DREAM   Y ❑   N ❑   Y ❑   N ❑

What is the message of the dream?

_____

_____

_____

_____

_____

_____

How does this affect you?

_____

_____

_____

_____

_____

LUCID TRIGGERS (identify patterns for next dream experience)

IDENTIFY SOMETHING SEEN **IDENTIFY SOMETHING HEARD** **IDENTIFY SOMETHING SMELLED**

IDENTIFY SOMETHING FELT **IDENTIFY SOMETHING TASTED** **SECRET TRIGGER PHRASE**

NAME YOUR DREAM **DATE**

/ /

WHO

Themes		Emotions
Birth ☐		☐ Amusement
Body Fears ☐		☐ Anger
Chased ☐		☐ Boldness
Defeat ☐		☐ Confusion
Disappearance ☐		☐ Courage
Disaster ☐		☐ Despair
Discovery ☐	WHAT	☐ Detachment
Driving ☐		☐ Envy
Falling ☐		☐ Fear
Flight ☐		☐ Happiness
Foreign Land ☐		☐ Hope
Money ☐		☐ Love
Nudity ☐		☐ Pity
Past Event ☐	WHERE	☐ Pleasure
Rejection ☐		☐ Pride
Sexual ☐		☐ Sadness
Stranger ☐		☐ Shame
Test ☐		☐ Stress
Threats ☐		☐ Surprise
_____ ☐		☐ Wonder

DRAW IMPORTANT DREAM IMAGERY (symbols, patterns, reoccurrences)

MAJOR RECENT EVENTS IN WAKING LIFE

RECURRING

Y ☐   N ☐

SHARE THIS DREAM

Y ☐   N ☐

LUCID DREAM

ANY CONNECTION TO DREAM   Y ☐   N ☐   Y ☐   N ☐

REFLECTIONS ON DREAM (follow your intuition)

What is the message of the dream?

_____

_____

_____

_____

_____

How does this affect you?

_____

_____

_____

_____

LUCID TRIGGERS (identify patterns for next dream experience)

IDENTIFY SOMETHING SEEN	IDENTIFY SOMETHING HEARD	IDENTIFY SOMETHING SMELLED
IDENTIFY SOMETHING FELT	IDENTIFY SOMETHING TASTED	SECRET TRIGGER PHRASE

NAME YOUR DREAM

DATE   /   /

WHO

Theme		Emotion
Birth ☐	_____	☐ Amusement
Body Fears ☐	_____	☐ Anger
Chased ☐	_____	☐ Boldness
Defeat ☐	_____	☐ Confusion
Disappearance ☐	_____	☐ Courage
Disaster ☐	_____	☐ Despair
Discovery ☐	WHAT	☐ Detachment
Driving ☐	_____	☐ Envy
Falling ☐	_____	☐ Fear
Flight ☐	_____	☐ Happiness
Foreign Land ☐	_____	☐ Hope
Money ☐	_____	☐ Love
Nudity ☐	_____	☐ Pity
Past Event ☐	WHERE	☐ Pleasure
Rejection ☐	_____	☐ Pride
Sexual ☐	_____	☐ Sadness
Stranger ☐	_____	☐ Shame
Test ☐	_____	☐ Stress
Threats ☐	_____	☐ Surprise
_____ ☐		☐ Wonder

DRAW IMPORTANT DREAM IMAGERY (symbols, patterns, reoccurrences)

MAJOR RECENT EVENTS IN WAKING LIFE

RECURRING

Y ☐   N ☐

SHARE THIS DREAM

Y ☐   N ☐

LUCID DREAM

ANY CONNECTION TO DREAM   Y ☐   N ☐   Y ☐   N ☐

What is the message of the dream?

_____
_____
_____
_____
_____
_____

How does this affect you?

_____
_____
_____
_____
_____

LUCID TRIGGERS (identify patterns for next dream experience)

IDENTIFY SOMETHING SEEN	IDENTIFY SOMETHING HEARD	IDENTIFY SOMETHING SMELLED

IDENTIFY SOMETHING FELT	IDENTIFY SOMETHING TASTED	SECRET TRIGGER PHRASE

NAME YOUR DREAM

DATE

/   /

WHO

Birth ❑	❑ Amusement
Body Fears ❑	❑ Anger
Chased ❑	❑ Boldness
Defeat ❑	❑ Confusion
Disappearance ❑	❑ Courage
Disaster ❑	❑ Despair
Discovery ❑	❑ Detachment
Driving ❑	❑ Envy
Falling ❑	❑ Fear
Flight ❑	❑ Happiness
Foreign Land ❑	❑ Hope
Money ❑	❑ Love
Nudity ❑	❑ Pity
Past Event ❑	❑ Pleasure
Rejection ❑	❑ Pride
Sexual ❑	❑ Sadness
Stranger ❑	❑ Shame
Test ❑	❑ Stress
Threats ❑	❑ Surprise
_____ ❑	❑ Wonder

WHAT

WHERE

DRAW IMPORTANT DREAM IMAGERY (symbols, patterns, reoccurrences)

MAJOR RECENT EVENTS IN WAKING LIFE

RECURRING

Y ❑   N ❑

SHARE THIS DREAM

Y ❑   N ❑

LUCID DREAM

ANY CONNECTION TO DREAM   Y ❑   N ❑   Y ❑   N ❑

What is the message of the dream?

_____

_____

_____

_____

_____

_____

How does this affect you?

_____

_____

_____

_____

_____

LUCID TRIGGERS (identify patterns for next dream experience)

IDENTIFY SOMETHING SEEN | **IDENTIFY SOMETHING HEARD** | **IDENTIFY SOMETHING SMELLED**

IDENTIFY SOMETHING FELT | **IDENTIFY SOMETHING TASTED** | **SECRET TRIGGER PHRASE**

NAME YOUR DREAM

DATE
/ /

WHO

THEMES		EMOTIONS
Birth ❑		❑ Amusement
Body Fears ❑		❑ Anger
Chased ❑		❑ Boldness
Defeat ❑		❑ Confusion
Disappearance ❑		❑ Courage
Disaster ❑		❑ Despair
Discovery ❑	**WHAT**	❑ Detachment
Driving ❑		❑ Envy
Falling ❑		❑ Fear
Flight ❑		❑ Happiness
Foreign Land ❑		❑ Hope
Money ❑		❑ Love
Nudity ❑		❑ Pity
Past Event ❑	**WHERE**	❑ Pleasure
Rejection ❑		❑ Pride
Sexual ❑		❑ Sadness
Stranger ❑		❑ Shame
Test ❑		❑ Stress
Threats ❑		❑ Surprise
_____ ❑		❑ Wonder

DRAW IMPORTANT DREAM IMAGERY (symbols, patterns, reoccurrences)

MAJOR RECENT EVENTS IN WAKING LIFE

RECURRING

Y ❑   N ❑

SHARE THIS DREAM

Y ❑   N ❑

LUCID DREAM

ANY CONNECTION TO DREAM   Y ❑   N ❑   Y ❑   N ❑

REFLECTIONS ON DREAM (follow your intuition)

What is the message of the dream?

_____

_____

_____

_____

_____

How does this affect you?

_____

_____

_____

_____

LUCID TRIGGERS (identify patterns for next dream experience)

IDENTIFY SOMETHING SEEN	IDENTIFY SOMETHING HEARD	IDENTIFY SOMETHING SMELLED
IDENTIFY SOMETHING FELT	IDENTIFY SOMETHING TASTED	SECRET TRIGGER PHRASE

NAME YOUR DREAM

DATE

/   /

WHO

Theme		Emotion
Birth ❑		❑ Amusement
Body Fears ❑		❑ Anger
Chased ❑		❑ Boldness
Defeat ❑		❑ Confusion
Disappearance ❑		❑ Courage
Disaster ❑		❑ Despair
Discovery ❑	**WHAT**	❑ Detachment
Driving ❑		❑ Envy
Falling ❑		❑ Fear
Flight ❑		❑ Happiness
Foreign Land ❑		❑ Hope
Money ❑		❑ Love
Nudity ❑		❑ Pity
Past Event ❑	**WHERE**	❑ Pleasure
Rejection ❑		❑ Pride
Sexual ❑		❑ Sadness
Stranger ❑		❑ Shame
Test ❑		❑ Stress
Threats ❑		❑ Surprise
_____ ❑		❑ Wonder

DRAW IMPORTANT DREAM IMAGERY (symbols, patterns, reoccurrences)

MAJOR RECENT EVENTS IN WAKING LIFE

_____

_____

_____

_____

RECURRING

Y ❑   N ❑

SHARE THIS DREAM

Y ❑   N ❑

LUCID DREAM

Y ❑   N ❑

ANY CONNECTION TO DREAM   Y ❑   N ❑

REFLECTIONS ON DREAM (follow your intuition)

What is the message of the dream?

_____

_____

_____

_____

_____

_____

How does this affect you?

_____

_____

_____

_____

_____

LUCID TRIGGERS (identify patterns for next dream experience)

IDENTIFY SOMETHING SEEN	IDENTIFY SOMETHING HEARD	IDENTIFY SOMETHING SMELLED
IDENTIFY SOMETHING FELT	IDENTIFY SOMETHING TASTED	SECRET TRIGGER PHRASE

NAME YOUR DREAM

DATE
/ /

WHO

THEMES		EMOTIONS
Birth ❑		❑ Amusement
Body Fears ❑		❑ Anger
Chased ❑		❑ Boldness
Defeat ❑		❑ Confusion
Disappearance ❑		❑ Courage
Disaster ❑		❑ Despair
Discovery ❑	WHAT	❑ Detachment
Driving ❑		❑ Envy
Falling ❑		❑ Fear
Flight ❑		❑ Happiness
Foreign Land ❑		❑ Hope
Money ❑		❑ Love
Nudity ❑		❑ Pity
Past Event ❑	WHERE	❑ Pleasure
Rejection ❑		❑ Pride
Sexual ❑		❑ Sadness
Stranger ❑		❑ Shame
Test ❑		❑ Stress
Threats ❑		❑ Surprise
_____ ❑		❑ Wonder

DRAW IMPORTANT DREAM IMAGERY (symbols, patterns, reoccurrences)

MAJOR RECENT EVENTS IN WAKING LIFE

RECURRING

Y ❑   N ❑

SHARE THIS DREAM

Y ❑   N ❑

LUCID DREAM

ANY CONNECTION TO DREAM   Y ❑   N ❑   Y ❑   N ❑

REFLECTIONS ON DREAM (follow your intuition)

What is the message of the dream?

_____

_____

_____

_____

_____

_____

How does this affect you?

_____

_____

_____

_____

LUCID TRIGGERS (identify patterns for next dream experience)

IDENTIFY SOMETHING SEEN	IDENTIFY SOMETHING HEARD	IDENTIFY SOMETHING SMELLED

IDENTIFY SOMETHING FELT	IDENTIFY SOMETHING TASTED	SECRET TRIGGER PHRASE

NAME YOUR DREAM

DATE

/ /

WHO

THEMES		EMOTIONS
Birth ❑		❑ Amusement
Body Fears ❑		❑ Anger
Chased ❑		❑ Boldness
Defeat ❑		❑ Confusion
Disappearance ❑		❑ Courage
Disaster ❑		❑ Despair
Discovery ❑	**WHAT**	❑ Detachment
Driving ❑		❑ Envy
Falling ❑		❑ Fear
Flight ❑		❑ Happiness
Foreign Land ❑		❑ Hope
Money ❑		❑ Love
Nudity ❑		❑ Pity
Past Event ❑	**WHERE**	❑ Pleasure
Rejection ❑		❑ Pride
Sexual ❑		❑ Sadness
Stranger ❑		❑ Shame
Test ❑		❑ Stress
Threats ❑		❑ Surprise
_____ ❑		❑ Wonder

DRAW IMPORTANT DREAM IMAGERY (symbols, patterns, reoccurrences)

MAJOR RECENT EVENTS IN WAKING LIFE

RECURRING

Y ❑   N ❑

SHARE THIS DREAM

Y ❑   N ❑

LUCID DREAM

ANY CONNECTION TO DREAM   Y ❑   N ❑   Y ❑   N ❑

REFLECTIONS ON DREAM (follow your intuition)

What is the message of the dream?

_____

_____

_____

_____

_____

How does this affect you?

_____

_____

_____

_____

LUCID TRIGGERS (identify patterns for next dream experience)

IDENTIFY SOMETHING SEEN	IDENTIFY SOMETHING HEARD	IDENTIFY SOMETHING SMELLED
IDENTIFY SOMETHING FELT	IDENTIFY SOMETHING TASTED	SECRET TRIGGER PHRASE

NAME YOUR DREAM

DATE

/ /

WHO

THEMES		EMOTIONS
Birth ❑		❑ Amusement
Body Fears ❑		❑ Anger
Chased ❑		❑ Boldness
Defeat ❑		❑ Confusion
Disappearance ❑		❑ Courage
Disaster ❑		❑ Despair
Discovery ❑	WHAT	❑ Detachment
Driving ❑		❑ Envy
Falling ❑		❑ Fear
Flight ❑		❑ Happiness
Foreign Land ❑		❑ Hope
Money ❑		❑ Love
Nudity ❑		❑ Pity
Past Event ❑	WHERE	❑ Pleasure
Rejection ❑		❑ Pride
Sexual ❑		❑ Sadness
Stranger ❑		❑ Shame
Test ❑		❑ Stress
Threats ❑		❑ Surprise
_____ ❑		❑ Wonder

DRAW IMPORTANT DREAM IMAGERY (symbols, patterns, reoccurrences)

MAJOR RECENT EVENTS IN WAKING LIFE

RECURRING

Y ❑   N ❑

SHARE THIS DREAM

Y ❑   N ❑

LUCID DREAM

Y ❑   N ❑

ANY CONNECTION TO DREAM   Y ❑   N ❑

What is the message of the dream?

_____
_____
_____
_____
_____
_____

How does this affect you?

_____
_____
_____
_____
_____

LUCID TRIGGERS (identify patterns for next dream experience)

IDENTIFY SOMETHING SEEN	IDENTIFY SOMETHING HEARD	IDENTIFY SOMETHING SMELLED
IDENTIFY SOMETHING FELT	**IDENTIFY SOMETHING TASTED**	**SECRET TRIGGER PHRASE**

NAME YOUR DREAM

DATE

/   /

WHO

THEMES		EMOTIONS
Birth ❑		❑ Amusement
Body Fears ❑		❑ Anger
Chased ❑		❑ Boldness
Defeat ❑		❑ Confusion
Disappearance ❑		❑ Courage
Disaster ❑		❑ Despair
Discovery ❑	**WHAT**	❑ Detachment
Driving ❑		❑ Envy
Falling ❑		❑ Fear
Flight ❑		❑ Happiness
Foreign Land ❑		❑ Hope
Money ❑		❑ Love
Nudity ❑		❑ Pity
Past Event ❑	**WHERE**	❑ Pleasure
Rejection ❑		❑ Pride
Sexual ❑		❑ Sadness
Stranger ❑		❑ Shame
Test ❑		❑ Stress
Threats ❑		❑ Surprise
_____ ❑		❑ Wonder

DRAW IMPORTANT DREAM IMAGERY (symbols, patterns, reoccurrences)

MAJOR RECENT EVENTS IN WAKING LIFE

RECURRING

Y ❑   N ❑

SHARE THIS DREAM

Y ❑   N ❑

LUCID DREAM

ANY CONNECTION TO DREAM   Y ❑   N ❑   Y ❑   N ❑

REFLECTIONS ON DREAM (follow your intuition)

What is the message of the dream?

_____

_____

_____

_____

_____

_____

How does this affect you?

_____

_____

_____

_____

LUCID TRIGGERS (identify patterns for next dream experience)

IDENTIFY SOMETHING SEEN	IDENTIFY SOMETHING HEARD	IDENTIFY SOMETHING SMELLED
IDENTIFY SOMETHING FELT	IDENTIFY SOMETHING TASTED	SECRET TRIGGER PHRASE

NAME YOUR DREAM

DATE

/   /

WHO

Birth ☐	———————————————	☐ Amusement
Body Fears ☐		☐ Anger
Chased ☐		☐ Boldness
Defeat ☐		☐ Confusion
Disappearance ☐		☐ Courage
Disaster ☐		☐ Despair
Discovery ☐	WHAT	☐ Detachment
Driving ☐		☐ Envy
Falling ☐		☐ Fear
Flight ☐		☐ Happiness
Foreign Land ☐		☐ Hope
Money ☐		☐ Love
Nudity ☐		☐ Pity
Past Event ☐	WHERE	☐ Pleasure
Rejection ☐		☐ Pride
Sexual ☐		☐ Sadness
Stranger ☐		☐ Shame
Test ☐		☐ Stress
Threats ☐		☐ Surprise
_____ ☐		☐ Wonder

DRAW IMPORTANT DREAM IMAGERY (symbols, patterns, reoccurrences)

MAJOR RECENT EVENTS IN WAKING LIFE

RECURRING

Y ☐   N ☐

SHARE THIS DREAM

Y ☐   N ☐

LUCID DREAM

ANY CONNECTION TO DREAM   Y ☐   N ☐   Y ☐   N ☐

REFLECTIONS ON DREAM (follow your intuition)

What is the message of the dream?

_____

_____

_____

_____

_____

How does this affect you?

_____

_____

_____

_____

LUCID TRIGGERS (identify patterns for next dream experience)

IDENTIFY SOMETHING SEEN

IDENTIFY SOMETHING HEARD

IDENTIFY SOMETHING SMELLED

IDENTIFY SOMETHING FELT

IDENTIFY SOMETHING TASTED

SECRET TRIGGER PHRASE

NAME YOUR DREAM

DATE

/   /

WHO

Birth ❑	_____	❑ Amusement
Body Fears ❑	_____	❑ Anger
Chased ❑	_____	❑ Boldness
Defeat ❑	_____	❑ Confusion
Disappearance ❑	_____	❑ Courage
Disaster ❑		❑ Despair
Discovery ❑	WHAT	❑ Detachment
Driving ❑	_____	❑ Envy
Falling ❑	_____	❑ Fear
Flight ❑	_____	❑ Happiness
Foreign Land ❑	_____	❑ Hope
Money ❑	_____	❑ Love
Nudity ❑	_____	❑ Pity
Past Event ❑	WHERE	❑ Pleasure
Rejection ❑	_____	❑ Pride
Sexual ❑	_____	❑ Sadness
Stranger ❑	_____	❑ Shame
Test ❑	_____	❑ Stress
Threats ❑	_____	❑ Surprise
_____ ❑		❑ Wonder

DRAW IMPORTANT DREAM IMAGERY (symbols, patterns, reoccurrences)

MAJOR RECENT EVENTS IN WAKING LIFE

RECURRING

Y ❑   N ❑

SHARE THIS DREAM

Y ❑   N ❑

LUCID DREAM

ANY CONNECTION TO DREAM   Y ❑   N ❑   Y ❑   N ❑

REFLECTIONS ON DREAM (follow your intuition)

What is the message of the dream?

_____

_____

_____

_____

_____

_____

How does this affect you?

_____

_____

_____

_____

LUCID TRIGGERS (identify patterns for next dream experience)

IDENTIFY SOMETHING SEEN	IDENTIFY SOMETHING HEARD	IDENTIFY SOMETHING SMELLED
IDENTIFY SOMETHING FELT	IDENTIFY SOMETHING TASTED	SECRET TRIGGER PHRASE

NAME YOUR DREAM

DATE

/ /

WHO

Birth ❑	
Body Fears ❑	
Chased ❑	
Defeat ❑	
Disappearance ❑	
Disaster ❑	
Discovery ❑	WHAT
Driving ❑	
Falling ❑	
Flight ❑	
Foreign Land ❑	
Money ❑	
Nudity ❑	
Past Event ❑	WHERE
Rejection ❑	
Sexual ❑	
Stranger ❑	
Test ❑	
Threats ❑	
_____ ❑	

EMOTIONS:

❑ Amusement
❑ Anger
❑ Boldness
❑ Confusion
❑ Courage
❑ Despair
❑ Detachment
❑ Envy
❑ Fear
❑ Happiness
❑ Hope
❑ Love
❑ Pity
❑ Pleasure
❑ Pride
❑ Sadness
❑ Shame
❑ Stress
❑ Surprise
❑ Wonder

DRAW IMPORTANT DREAM IMAGERY (symbols, patterns, reoccurrences)

MAJOR RECENT EVENTS IN WAKING LIFE

RECURRING

Y ❑   N ❑

SHARE THIS DREAM

Y ❑   N ❑

LUCID DREAM

ANY CONNECTION TO DREAM   Y ❑   N ❑   Y ❑   N ❑

REFLECTIONS ON DREAM (follow your intuition)

What is the message of the dream?

_____

_____

_____

_____

_____

_____

How does this affect you?

_____

_____

_____

_____

LUCID TRIGGERS (identify patterns for next dream experience)

IDENTIFY SOMETHING SEEN	IDENTIFY SOMETHING HEARD	IDENTIFY SOMETHING SMELLED
IDENTIFY SOMETHING FELT	**IDENTIFY SOMETHING TASTED**	**SECRET TRIGGER PHRASE**

NAME YOUR DREAM

DATE

/   /

WHO

THEMES		EMOTIONS
Birth ☐		☐ Amusement
Body Fears ☐		☐ Anger
Chased ☐		☐ Boldness
Defeat ☐		☐ Confusion
Disappearance ☐		☐ Courage
Disaster ☐		☐ Despair
Discovery ☐	WHAT	☐ Detachment
Driving ☐		☐ Envy
Falling ☐		☐ Fear
Flight ☐		☐ Happiness
Foreign Land ☐		☐ Hope
Money ☐		☐ Love
Nudity ☐		☐ Pity
Past Event ☐	WHERE	☐ Pleasure
Rejection ☐		☐ Pride
Sexual ☐		☐ Sadness
Stranger ☐		☐ Shame
Test ☐		☐ Stress
Threats ☐		☐ Surprise
_____ ☐		☐ Wonder

DRAW IMPORTANT DREAM IMAGERY (symbols, patterns, reoccurrences)

MAJOR RECENT EVENTS IN WAKING LIFE

RECURRING

Y ☐   N ☐

SHARE THIS DREAM

Y ☐   N ☐

LUCID DREAM

ANY CONNECTION TO DREAM   Y ☐   N ☐   Y ☐   N ☐

REFLECTIONS ON DREAM (follow your intuition)

What is the message of the dream?

_____

_____

_____

_____

_____

How does this affect you?

_____

_____

_____

_____

LUCID TRIGGERS (identify patterns for next dream experience)

IDENTIFY SOMETHING SEEN	IDENTIFY SOMETHING HEARD	IDENTIFY SOMETHING SMELLED
IDENTIFY SOMETHING FELT	IDENTIFY SOMETHING TASTED	SECRET TRIGGER PHRASE

NAME YOUR DREAM

DATE

/   /

WHO

Birth ❑	
Body Fears ❑	
Chased ❑	
Defeat ❑	
Disappearance ❑	
Disaster ❑	
Discovery ❑	
Driving ❑	
Falling ❑	
Flight ❑	
Foreign Land ❑	
Money ❑	
Nudity ❑	
Past Event ❑	
Rejection ❑	
Sexual ❑	
Stranger ❑	
Test ❑	
Threats ❑	
_____ ❑	

WHAT

WHERE

❑ Amusement
❑ Anger
❑ Boldness
❑ Confusion
❑ Courage
❑ Despair
❑ Detachment
❑ Envy
❑ Fear
❑ Happiness
❑ Hope
❑ Love
❑ Pity
❑ Pleasure
❑ Pride
❑ Sadness
❑ Shame
❑ Stress
❑ Surprise
❑ Wonder

DRAW IMPORTANT DREAM IMAGERY (symbols, patterns, reoccurrences)

MAJOR RECENT EVENTS IN WAKING LIFE

RECURRING

Y ❑   N ❑

SHARE THIS DREAM

Y ❑   N ❑

LUCID DREAM

ANY CONNECTION TO DREAM   Y ❑   N ❑   Y ❑   N ❑

REFLECTIONS ON DREAM (follow your intuition)

What is the message of the dream?

_____

_____

_____

_____

_____

How does this affect you?

_____

_____

_____

_____

LUCID TRIGGERS (identify patterns for next dream experience)

IDENTIFY SOMETHING SEEN	IDENTIFY SOMETHING HEARD	IDENTIFY SOMETHING SMELLED
IDENTIFY SOMETHING FELT	IDENTIFY SOMETHING TASTED	SECRET TRIGGER PHRASE

NAME YOUR DREAM

DATE

/ /

How to Use This Journal

This journal was designed to help you fully explore your dreams, whether to lucid dream or interpret them. That said, this journal like any other journal can be used in the manner of your choosing. You can use slots in different ways or ignore them altogether. But this quick overview will cover the most common ways of using this journal.

Section 1: Immediate Recall

This is best completed immediately after waking from a dream. The Who, What, Where sections can be used to jot quickly down dream details. Be specific but no more than necessary. They key here is getting as much of the full dream experience as possible.

Next identify themes and emotions. There's often more than one and linking them to key moments in the dream can help you to identify reoccurring patterns.

THEMES	QUICK DREAM RECALL	EMOTIONS
Birth ☒	**WHO** First I saw Roger from work	☐ Amusement
Body Fears ☐	Later I saw Aunty Betty	☐ Anger
Chased ☐	Stranger holding balloons	☐ Boldness
Defeat ☐	Tall basketball player	☒ Confusion
Disappearance ☐	Steve Martin?	☐ Courage
Disaster ☐		☐ Despair
Discovery ☐	**WHAT** I was at a work party and Roger was retiring.	☐ Detachment
Driving ☐	For some reason I found Aunt Betty in the lunch	☐ Envy
Falling ☐	room talking to a man holding balloons. Later this	☒ Fear
Flight ☐	really tall basketball player came in and said my car	☒ Happiness
Foreign Land ☐	was being towed away by STEVE MARTIN. What!	☐ Hope
Money ☐		☐ Love
Nudity ☐		☐ Pity
Past Event ☒	**WHERE** I started off in Roger's office but later went to the	☒ Pleasure
Rejection ☐	lunch room, which looked like my parent's bedroom	☐ Pride
Sexual ☐	as a kid. The parking lot was actually the parking lot	☐ Sadness
Stranger ☒	from the bookstore down the street.	☐ Shame
Test ☐		☒ Stress
Threats ☐		☒ Surprise
_____ ☐		☐ Wonder

Section 2: Dream Imagery

Your drawing skills don't matter here. What matters here is identifying imagery that strikes you as important. That can be something that is heavy in symbolism, or events/objects that make up a pattern or that regularly appear. Jot down your impressions as well.

DRAW IMPORTANT DREAM IMAGERY (symbols, patterns, reoccurrences)

Roger was retiring but he was blowing out a birthday cake.

More birtday imagery

Basketball players jersey had my birth year.

Section 3: External Summary

Next you'll want to identify major events surrounding your life. These events need not be life-altering, but that simply have significance and are personally meaningful to you. Try to decide whether this dream is connected to any of those events.

Then answer these quick questions:

Is this a reoccurring dream?

Is this a dream you would be willing to share with others for pleasure or better understanding?

Was this a lucid dream? Did you become conscious at any point?

MAJOR RECENT EVENTS IN WAKING LIFE

Just turned 35 years old

Didn't get that promotion.

I've been stressing about my future.

RECURRING

Y ☐   N ☒

SHARE THIS DREAM

Y ☒   N ☐

LUCID DREAM

Y ☐   N ☒

ANY CONNECTION TO DREAM   Y ☒   N ☐

Section 4: Personal Reflection

Now is your chance to think about the meaning of your dream. Your intuition will be key here since dreams are inherently deeply personal experiences. They are essentially stories you are telling yourself. Challenge yourself to find a message, but don't overly impose meaning on it. Think: Is there something I'm trying to teach myself?

If you discover a meaningful message, ask yourself how this can be beneficial to your waking life. Does it offer clarity or wisdom to something you're striving to overcome? How can you apply this new understanding to your life?

REFLECTIONS ON DREAM (follow your intuition)

What is the message of the dream?

I think this was about my worry over turning 35 and still not having a clear indication of how my life will turn out. But I also think that Aunty Betty symbolized hope. She always said not to worry too much about my future. She made feel confident. Can't yet explain the basketball player but I think Steve Martin was another good sign. I was happy to see him even though he was towing my car. I remember now him saying, "Its OK. You just need a tune up."

How does this affect you?

I think it's time to let go of some of that fear regarding my future. Even though I didn't get the promotion, Erin did say it was a tough decision and that I'd be first up next time.

Section 5: Lucid Triggers

The more you analyze and identify curious dream phenomenons, the better you'll become at lucid dreaming. Record key sensory details that clearly oppose reality. This practice will prime you for later lucid dreaming.

Secret Trigger Phrase

Plant a seed in your subconscious. Practice saying the phrase during waking hours and ask yourself: "Am I dreaming?" Follow this up by reality checking your environment. Does your watch read right? Do words on signs change or disappear? If so, you may be dreaming!

IDENTIFY SOMETHING SEEN	IDENTIFY SOMETHING HEARD	IDENTIFY SOMETHING SMELLED
The painting in the lunch room was on a wall in my parent's bedroom.	Aunty Betty's giggle in the lunch room.	None come to mind.

IDENTIFY SOMETHING FELT	IDENTIFY SOMETHING TASTED	SECRET TRIGGER PHRASE
The parking lot ground had a sticky ground.	The birthday cake was really gooey.	This sweater needs more toothpaste!

Section 5: Name Your Dream

This last part may seem trivial but in fact it's so important that we placed it at the end. Generally, titles go at the beginning but the truth is you often don't know what a dream actually reflects until after you've spent time exploring it. Only then do you arrive at an "Aha" moment. This may not always happen, but you'll be better able to label your dream after you've fully explored it.

NAME YOUR DREAM	DATE
Birthday Worries Be Gone	8 / 5 / 15

Now Go and Explore Your Dreams!

Join other dreamers at on our Facebook page

 LUCID DREAMING SOCIETY

Made in the USA
Middletown, DE
04 June 2017